MAXIMIZING
VENDING SUCCESS

A Practical Guide to Improving
Vending Opportunities

**BY: DR. CLEMENT KWAKYE
& SAMEERAH KWAKYE**

TABLE OF CONTENTS

2. Email Marketing

3. Collaborate with Event Organizers

4. Flyers and Posters

Marketing During the Event

1. Live Social Media Coverage

2. In-Booth Promotions and Giveaways

3. Capture Customer Information

Marketing After the Event

1. Post-Event Thank You and Follow-Up Emails

2. Share Event Highlights on Social Media

3. Customer Testimonials and Reviews

4. Prepare for the Next Event

Conclusion: A Holistic Approach to Vending Marketing

1. Navigating Bad Weather

Preparation is Key

Weather-Responsive Adjustments

Weather-Specific Promotions

2. Managing Low Foot Traffic

Maximize Every Opportunity

Adjust Expectations

Optimize Slow Periods

3. Dealing with Unexpected Competition

Focus on Your Strengths

Stay Positive and Collaborative

4. Overcoming Logistical and Operational Issues

Be Prepared with Backup Plans

Chapter 1: Understanding the Basics of Vending Success

- Overview of vending as a business model
- Different types of vending opportunities (markets, fairs, pop-up events, permanent locations)
- Key factors that contribute to a successful vending business
- Identifying your goals: profitability, brand exposure, customer engagement

Chapter 2: Researching and Choosing the Right Vending Events

- How to research vending events that align with your business goals
- Understanding your target audience and selecting events that attract them
- Evaluating event organizers, vendors, and past performance of events
- How to apply for vending opportunities and secure your spot

Chapter 3: Creating an Eye-Catching Vending Setup

- Designing a visually appealing booth that attracts customers
- Tips on branding your vending space (signage, colors, layout)
- Maximizing space and organizing your products effectively
- Importance of lighting, display, and cleanliness for customer experience

Chapter 4: Setting the Right Price and Payment Options

- Pricing strategies that attract buyers and ensure profitability
- Understanding your cost structure and factoring in overheads (vendor fees, transportation)
- Offering discounts, bundles, or limited-time offers to encourage purchases
- Exploring payment options: cash, mobile payment apps, credit/debit cards

Chapter 5: Inventory Management for Vending Events

- How to predict demand and stock the right amount of products
- Importance of tracking inventory before, during, and after events
- Strategies for restocking popular items and managing slow-moving products
- Planning for bulk orders and seasonal shifts in demand

Chapter 6: Engaging Customers and Driving Sales

- Best practices for approaching and engaging customers at your booth
- The art of conversation: how to balance friendliness with professional sales tactics
- Offering demonstrations or free samples to increase interest
- How to upsell and cross-sell without being pushy

Chapter 7: Navigating Competition at Vending Events

- How to differentiate your booth and products from competitors

- Competitive pricing strategies without compromising profitability
- Building customer loyalty through unique product offerings or personalized service
- Using event networking to collaborate with other vendors

Chapter 8: Marketing Before, During, and After Vending Events

- Promoting your vending appearances through social media, email, and local advertising
- Using event hashtags and geotags to draw attention on social media
- Collecting customer emails and contact info for follow-up marketing
- Turning vending events into long-term customer relationships and repeat business

Chapter 9: Handling Challenges and Setbacks

- Preparing for unexpected problems like bad weather, low foot traffic, or technical issues
- How to stay flexible and make quick adjustments during events
- Dealing with negative customer interactions professionally
- Evaluating event performance and learning from challenges to improve future vending opportunities

Chapter 10: Scaling Your Vending Business

- When and how to expand to new locations or larger events
- Leveraging online platforms to supplement your vending business

- Exploring partnerships, collaborations, and sponsorships to enhance exposure
- Strategies for growing your customer base beyond vending events

INTRODUCTION

YOUR GUIDE TO VENDING SUCCESS

The world of vending is an exciting yet challenging landscape, where passion, creativity, and business savvy intersect. Whether you're a seasoned vendor or just starting out, achieving success in this competitive space requires more than simply setting up a booth and displaying your products. True success lies in a blend of strategic planning, customer engagement, adaptability, and continuous growth. This book is designed to be your comprehensive guide to navigating the unique demands of vending, equipping you with the tools and insights needed to stand out, attract loyal customers, and scale your business effectively.

From bustling farmers markets and craft fairs to pop-up events and holiday bazaars, vending offers diverse opportunities to showcase your products, connect with your audience, and build a brand that resonates. However, these events also come with their own set of challenges—unpredictable weather, competition from other vendors, managing inventory, and more. To thrive in such an environment, you need a solid foundation, clear goals, and the flexibility to adapt to changing conditions. This book will walk you through every aspect of building and growing a successful vending business, step by step.

In the first chapters, we'll begin with the essentials: understanding the basics of vending, choosing the right events, and creating an eye-catching setup that draws customers in. You'll learn how to research vending opportunities, identify your target market, and design a booth that not only looks appealing but also reflects your unique brand. We'll discuss the importance of pricing your products strategically and offering flexible payment options to maximize sales.

Customer engagement is at the heart of a successful vending business, and we dedicate a chapter to mastering the art of connecting with customers. From the initial greeting to handling questions and objections, we'll cover techniques to build meaningful relationships with potential buyers, turning casual browsers into loyal customers. Building these connections not only boosts your sales but also strengthens your reputation, laying the groundwork for repeat business and word-of-mouth referrals.

But vending isn't always smooth sailing. You'll inevitably encounter challenges, whether it's competing vendors, low foot traffic, or logistical setbacks. This book provides practical strategies for overcoming these obstacles with confidence. You'll learn how to differentiate yourself from the competition, make the most of slow periods, and handle unexpected setbacks without losing momentum. By embracing a proactive mindset, you can turn challenges into opportunities for growth.

As you build a strong foundation, the final chapters will guide you through scaling your business for long-term success. Expanding to new locations, diversifying your product offerings, and leveraging online platforms are all ways to reach a broader audience and increase revenue. You'll gain insights into creating an e-commerce presence, attending larger events, and streamlining your operations for efficiency. Scaling your business takes careful planning and commitment, but the rewards can be substantial.

This book is not just a guide—it's a toolkit, filled with actionable advice and strategies to help you succeed in every aspect of vending. Each chapter is crafted to provide you with the knowledge, skills, and confidence to make informed decisions and maximize your opportunities. Whether you're looking to make vending a full-time business or an enjoyable side venture, this book will empower you to turn your passion into a profitable, thriving enterprise.

Welcome to your journey toward vending success. Let's dive in and unlock the potential that awaits!

CHAPTER 1

UNDERSTANDING THE BASICS OF VENDING SUCCESS

Vending can be a highly rewarding business model for entrepreneurs looking to showcase their products in a dynamic, face-to-face environment. Whether you're vending at farmers markets, craft fairs, pop-up events, or permanent vending locations, success is often dependent on understanding the key elements that drive sales, customer engagement, and brand recognition. This chapter lays the foundation for your vending journey by outlining the essential components of vending success, explaining different types of vending opportunities, and helping you clarify your goals to ensure long-term profitability and growth.

The Fundamentals of Vending Success

Vending involves more than just setting up a table and waiting for customers to buy your products. It's about creating an inviting, engaging space where potential customers feel compelled to stop, browse, and ultimately make a purchase. To achieve this, you need to consider the following core elements of vending success:

1. **Product**: The first and most important factor in your vending business is what you sell. Whether it's handmade jewelry, gourmet food items, or artisanal crafts, your product needs to stand out. Successful vendors understand their product inside and out, ensuring that it meets the needs and desires of their target customers. It's also essential that your product is well-made, competitively priced, and unique enough to attract attention in a crowded marketplace.

2. **Presentation**: How you present your product is key to drawing in customers. This goes beyond the physical display at your booth to include packaging, branding, and even how you and your staff (if applicable) interact with customers. People are often attracted to well-organized, visually appealing displays. Your booth should reflect your brand's personality and be instantly recognizable, helping to differentiate you from the competition.

3. **Engagement**: Vending success is highly dependent on how well you engage with your customers. People are more likely to purchase from a vendor who is friendly, knowledgeable, and approachable. Great customer service can set you apart, especially if you're in a competitive vending environment. Engaging with customers also provides valuable insights into what they like, what they're looking for, and how you can improve your offerings.

4. **Location**: The old adage "location, location, location" holds true for vending. The success of your booth is often determined by where it is situated within an event or market. High foot traffic areas, spots near entrances, and locations that are easy to find all increase the likelihood that potential customers will stop by. It's also important to research the events and markets where you're vending to ensure that your target demographic will be in attendance.

5. **Consistency**: Vending is not a "set it and forget it" operation. It requires continuous effort and refinement. Regularly attending events, consistently delivering high-quality products, and maintaining an inviting booth setup are crucial to building a loyal customer base. Consistency in your branding, product offerings, and customer service ensures that people recognize your business and know what to expect.

Types of Vending Opportunities

Not all vending opportunities are created equal, and understanding the different types available will help you choose the right one for your business. Each vending opportunity has its unique advantages and challenges, so it's important to select those that align with your goals and target audience.

1. **Farmers Markets**: Farmers markets typically feature vendors selling fresh produce, handmade goods, artisanal foods, and natural products. These markets are usually held weekly or biweekly and tend to attract local, community-oriented customers. Vendors at farmers markets benefit from regular exposure to loyal customers who value high-quality, locally sourced products. However, competition can be fierce, and booth fees, though typically lower than larger events, can add up over time.

2. **Craft Fairs and Art Shows**: Craft fairs and art shows are ideal for vendors who specialize in handmade or artistic products. These events often attract an audience looking for one-of-a-kind items, such as jewelry, artwork, home decor, or clothing. Craft fairs vary in size, from small local events to large, regional festivals. The key to success at these events is having a unique product and an eye-catching booth that draws in customers.

3. **Pop-Up Events**: Pop-up markets are temporary retail opportunities that usually occur for a limited time (e.g., a day, a weekend, or a holiday season). These events are often held in high-traffic locations like urban areas, shopping centers, or during special community events. Pop-up markets allow vendors to test new products, explore different locations, and capitalize on seasonal or event-based trends. They can be an excellent option for

vendors looking to make a short-term impact without committing to a permanent space.

4. **Festivals and Fairs**: Large-scale festivals, fairs, and street markets can attract thousands of attendees, offering significant sales opportunities for vendors. These events range from food festivals and music concerts to cultural fairs and holiday markets. The high foot traffic at festivals can lead to substantial sales, but booth fees are often higher, and competition among vendors is more intense. These events are best suited for vendors who are prepared to handle large crowds and have the inventory to meet high demand.

5. **Permanent Vending Locations**: Some vendors opt for a permanent vending location, such as a kiosk in a mall, a food truck, or a booth in a year-round market. Permanent vending offers stability and the ability to build a consistent customer base, but it also requires a significant upfront investment and ongoing overhead costs. It's a great option for vendors who are ready to commit to a specific location and product offering.

6. **Trade Shows and Expos**: Trade shows and expos are specialized events that cater to specific industries or niches, such as health and wellness, food, fashion, or technology. These events are typically geared toward B2B (business-to-business) or B2C (business-to-consumer) interactions. While trade shows can be expensive to attend, they offer valuable networking opportunities and exposure to a targeted audience that is interested in your product category.

Defining Your Goals as a Vendor

Before diving into the vending world, it's essential to clarify your goals. Understanding what you want to achieve with your vending business will guide your decision-making process and help you stay focused on the right opportunities. Here are a few key questions to help you define your vending goals:

1. **Profitability**: Is your primary goal to generate income? If so, you'll need to focus on events with high foot traffic, where your target audience is likely to be present. This will also influence how you price your products, manage inventory, and structure your booth. Profit-driven vendors often focus on high-demand products, competitive pricing, and maximizing sales volume.

2. **Brand Exposure**: Some vendors are less focused on immediate profit and more interested in building brand recognition. If your goal is to gain exposure, you may be willing to attend events where sales are lower but networking opportunities are higher. These vendors prioritize getting their name out there, engaging with customers, and leaving a lasting impression to build future business opportunities.

3. **Customer Engagement and Feedback**: For newer vendors or those launching a new product, attending vending events can be an opportunity to engage with potential customers and gather valuable feedback. By interacting with customers, you can learn more about their preferences, adjust your product offering, and refine your branding.

4. **Community Involvement**: Some vendors are motivated by the desire to engage with their local community and build relationships. If this is your goal, participating in local

farmers markets, fairs, and charity events can be a great way to establish a local presence and foster a loyal customer base.

5. **Scaling Your Business**: For vendors looking to grow their business beyond local markets and events, vending can be a stepping stone toward scaling up. You may attend larger events, explore pop-up locations in new cities, or use vending as a way to test different markets before expanding to online retail or brick-and-mortar stores.

Conclusion: The First Step to Vending Success

Understanding the basics of vending success is the first step in building a thriving vending business. By focusing on the core elements—your product, presentation, engagement, location, and consistency—you can create an inviting, professional booth that attracts customers and drives sales. Furthermore, selecting the right vending opportunities and defining clear goals for your business will set you on the path to long-term success.

As you move through the rest of this book, you'll dive deeper into the practical strategies and techniques needed to refine your vending approach, improve your sales, and grow your customer base. With a solid foundation in place, you're ready to tackle the exciting and rewarding world of vending with confidence and clarity.

CHAPTER 2

RESEARCHING AND CHOOSING THE RIGHT VENDING EVENTS

One of the most critical decisions you'll make as a vendor is choosing the right vending events to attend. Not all events are created equal, and the success of your vending business often hinges on selecting events that align with your goals, product offerings, and target audience. In this chapter, we'll delve into the importance of researching vending opportunities, how to evaluate events to ensure they are a good fit for your business, and what factors to consider when deciding where to set up shop.

By carefully selecting the right events, you can maximize your sales, build meaningful relationships with customers, and strengthen your brand presence. Making the wrong choice, however, can lead to wasted time, money, and effort. This chapter will provide a comprehensive guide to help you make informed decisions about which vending events to attend.

Researching Potential Vending Events

Once you've identified the types of vending events that align with your product and goals, it's time to research specific events to ensure they're a good fit. Here are several key steps to help you effectively research and choose the right vending opportunities:

1. **Assess Your Target Audience**: Understanding your target audience is essential for choosing the right events. Different types of events attract different demographics, so it's important to select events that cater to the customers who are most likely to be interested in your

products. Consider factors such as age, income level, interests, and buying habits. For example, if you sell high-end artisanal crafts, you'll want to attend events where customers are willing to spend more on handmade items.

2. **Research Event Organizers**: Look into the reputation of the event organizers. Events run by experienced, well-established organizers are more likely to attract a large, engaged crowd and offer a seamless experience for vendors. Check if the organizers have a history of running successful events and look for feedback from other vendors who have attended in the past. You can often find reviews or testimonials on social media, event websites, or online forums.

3. **Examine Past Event Performance**: A great way to evaluate an event's potential is by reviewing past performance. Many events post photos, videos, and attendance numbers from previous years, giving you an idea of what to expect in terms of foot traffic, audience engagement, and overall atmosphere. If possible, attend the event as a visitor before committing as a vendor. This allows you to observe the layout, crowd dynamics, and competition firsthand.

4. **Consider the Event's Theme or Focus**: Pay attention to the theme or focus of the event. Some events are highly specialized, targeting specific interests such as eco-friendly products, gourmet food, or handmade crafts. If your products align with the event's theme, you'll likely have a better chance of attracting customers who are genuinely interested in what you offer. Conversely, vending at an event that doesn't align with your product could result in poor sales and wasted effort.

5. **Analyze Booth Costs and Fees**: Booth fees can vary significantly depending on the size, location, and prestige

of the event. While larger events with high foot traffic might offer more sales opportunities, they also come with higher costs. Consider your budget carefully and calculate how much inventory you'll need to sell to cover the booth fee and make a profit. Don't forget to factor in additional costs like transportation, accommodations, and supplies.

6. **Check Event Logistics**: Before committing to an event, ensure that the logistics work for you. Consider factors such as the location's accessibility (for both you and your customers), setup and teardown times, parking availability, and whether the event provides electricity, water, or other amenities. Additionally, review any rules or restrictions for vendors, such as product limitations, payment requirements, or promotional regulations.

7. **Vendor Competition**: Take note of how many other vendors will be attending the event and what they will be selling. If the market is oversaturated with vendors offering similar products to yours, it may be difficult to stand out or make a significant profit. However, if the event features a curated selection of vendors with minimal overlap, your chances of success increase. Some event organizers publish a list of attending vendors, which can help you assess the level of competition.

Evaluating Event Fit for Your Business

After conducting your research, it's time to evaluate whether a specific event is a good fit for your business. Use the following criteria to guide your decision:

1. **Audience Alignment**: Does the event attract your target audience? Are the attendees likely to be interested in your product and willing to spend money on it? An event may be large and well-attended, but if the audience doesn't

align with your product, you may not see the sales you expect.

2. **Sales Potential**: What is the event's sales potential, and does it justify the costs? Consider the expected foot traffic, the buying behavior of the attendees, and how much competition you'll face. Estimate how much inventory you'll need to sell to break even and make a profit. If the numbers don't add up, it might be worth looking at alternative events.

3. **Brand Exposure**: Even if an event doesn't promise high immediate sales, it could still be valuable for brand exposure. If you're trying to grow your customer base or raise awareness about your business, attending events that draw large crowds or media attention can be beneficial. Be sure to weigh the long-term benefits of brand exposure against the short-term sales potential.

4. **Networking Opportunities**: Some events offer valuable networking opportunities with other vendors, potential collaborators, or industry influencers. If you're looking to build relationships, expand your business network, or learn from other experienced vendors, these opportunities can be just as important as sales. Trade shows, expos, and festivals often provide a chance to connect with others in your industry.

Making the Final Decision

After evaluating the various aspects of each event, you'll need to make a final decision about where to focus your efforts. Choose events that align with your goals, budget, and target audience, and remember that not every event will be a perfect fit. It's better to attend fewer, high-quality events that generate meaningful sales and engagement than to spread yourself too thin by attending every event you come across.

Conclusion: Strategic Vending Event Selection

Choosing the right vending event is one of the most important decisions you'll make as a vendor. With careful research, thorough evaluation, and a clear understanding of your business goals, you can select events that maximize your sales potential, strengthen your brand presence, and help you grow your customer base. By attending the right events, you'll set yourself up for long-term vending success and ensure that each opportunity contributes positively to your business journey.

In the next chapter, we'll explore how to create an eye-catching vending setup that draws customers to your booth and enhances your chances of making sales.

CHAPTER 3

CREATING AN EYE-CATCHING VENDING SETUP

In the world of vending, your setup plays a crucial role in attracting customers and making sales. It's often said that people buy with their eyes first, and your booth's appearance is the first impression potential customers have of your business. A well-designed, eye-catching vending setup can set you apart from competitors, draw in foot traffic, and create a memorable experience that encourages people to buy. In this chapter, we'll discuss how to design an appealing booth that effectively showcases your products, aligns with your brand, and invites customers to engage with your business.

The Power of First Impressions

In a busy market or event setting, customers are often overwhelmed by the number of vendors vying for their attention. With so many options, it's easy for people to walk by your booth without stopping. This is why first impressions are so important. Within seconds, potential customers will decide whether your booth is worth a closer look, based primarily on its visual appeal and how approachable it feels.

To create a strong first impression, focus on the following elements:

1. **Visual Appeal**: Your booth should be visually engaging and reflective of your brand's personality. Bright colors, attractive displays, and well-organized products can instantly capture attention. Avoid clutter, as it can be overwhelming and make it difficult for customers to see

what you're offering. Instead, aim for a clean, streamlined look that highlights your best products.

2. **Brand Consistency**: Consistency in branding across your booth's design, signage, and product packaging helps build recognition and trust. Use the same colors, fonts, and logos that you use in your other marketing materials, such as your website or business cards. This consistency ensures that customers immediately know who you are and what you stand for, which can help build brand loyalty.

3. **Product Display**: How you display your products matters just as much as the products themselves. Your booth should be designed to showcase your items in the best possible light. Use different heights, textures, and arrangements to create an appealing display that encourages customers to explore your offerings. Consider using shelves, risers, or racks to add dimension and make your booth feel more dynamic.

4. **Clear Signage**: People need to know what you're selling, how much it costs, and any special deals or promotions. Clear, professional signage is essential for conveying this information. Your signage should be easy to read from a distance and consistent with your brand's design. Avoid handwritten signs, as they can look unprofessional, unless they fit with your brand's aesthetic. Digital or printed signage tends to look more polished.

Designing Your Booth Layout

The layout of your booth is critical to guiding customer flow and encouraging interaction with your products. A well-thought-out layout can make it easy for customers to browse, discover new items, and make a purchase. Consider the following tips when designing your booth layout:

1. **Maximize Space**: Whether you have a small table or a larger booth space, it's important to make the most of the area you have. Use vertical space to display products by adding shelving or racks. If your booth is located outdoors, consider using a canopy or tent to provide shelter from the elements while also giving you more space to display signage and branding.

2. **Create an Inviting Entrance**: Your booth's entrance should be open and inviting, encouraging customers to come in and browse. Avoid blocking the front of your booth with tables or displays, as this can create a barrier between you and your potential customers. Instead, position yourself and your key products near the front to welcome people in.

3. **Use Flow to Your Advantage**: Think about how customers will move through your booth. If possible, create a flow that guides them from one product to the next, similar to the way a well-designed retail store encourages customers to explore. Make sure there is enough space for people to move comfortably without feeling crowded.

4. **Highlight Key Products**: Place your most popular or eye-catching items at the front of your booth, where they are easily visible to passersby. Use additional lighting or special displays to draw attention to these items. By featuring your best products, you can spark interest and entice customers to come in and see what else you have to offer.

Lighting and Atmosphere

Lighting is an often-overlooked aspect of booth design, but it can have a big impact on the overall atmosphere and appeal of your setup. Good lighting not only makes your booth look more professional but also highlights your products and creates a warm, inviting atmosphere.

1. **Use Lighting to Enhance Products**: Proper lighting can make your products stand out, especially at indoor or evening events where natural light is limited. Use spotlights or string lights to highlight specific items, such as featured products or high-margin items. Soft lighting can create a welcoming environment, while brighter lighting can draw attention to special displays or signs.

2. **Create a Cohesive Atmosphere**: The atmosphere of your booth should align with your brand. If you sell eco-friendly or handmade products, for example, a natural, earthy vibe with soft, warm lighting may resonate with your customers. On the other hand, if you sell high-tech gadgets, bright, modern lighting may be more appropriate. Tailor your lighting and overall atmosphere to create a space that reflects your brand identity.

3. **Consider the Time of Day**: If you're vending at an outdoor market that runs into the evening, make sure your booth is well-lit as it gets dark. String lights, battery-powered lamps, or even LED lights can help ensure that your products remain visible and appealing to customers as the day progresses.

Engaging Your Senses

While sight is the primary sense you'll engage with your booth's visual design, don't forget about the other senses—especially smell, sound, and touch. Creating a multisensory experience can make your booth more memorable and enjoyable for customers, encouraging them to spend more time browsing and interacting with your products.

1. **Smell**: If your products have a pleasant scent (such as candles, soaps, or food), make sure the fragrance is noticeable but not overpowering. For vendors selling food items, the smell of freshly prepared food can be an incredibly powerful way to draw people in. Even if your products aren't scented, you can use a light, pleasant fragrance in your booth to create a welcoming atmosphere.

2. **Sound**: Background music can help set the mood and create a more inviting space. Choose music that aligns with your brand and enhances the overall experience without being too loud or distracting. Soft, ambient music works well in most cases, while more upbeat music might be appropriate for lively, high-energy events.

3. **Touch**: Encourage customers to interact with your products by making them easily accessible and inviting to touch. For example, if you sell clothing, make sure the fabrics are within reach for customers to feel. If you sell art or home decor, consider having samples or display pieces that customers can handle to get a better sense of their quality.

Branding Your Booth

Your booth setup is an extension of your brand, and it should reflect your brand's personality, values, and style. Strong branding helps customers remember you and encourages them to associate your products with positive experiences. Here are some ways to incorporate branding into your booth setup:

1. **Use Consistent Colors and Themes**: Your booth should use the same colors, fonts, and design elements that you use across your marketing materials, such as your website, social media profiles, and packaging. This consistency

reinforces your brand identity and makes it easier for customers to recognize you, even at different events.

2. **Add Personal Touches**: Personalizing your booth can create a stronger connection with customers. Whether it's a handwritten thank-you note for each purchase, a story about how your products are made, or photos of your creative process, adding personal elements to your booth helps customers connect with you as an individual, not just a business.

3. **Branded Merchandise and Packaging**: Offering branded merchandise, such as tote bags or T-shirts, can extend your brand beyond the event and provide additional exposure. Similarly, use branded packaging for all purchases, so that even after the event is over, customers will be reminded of your business when they see your packaging at home.

Interactive Elements and Promotions

Adding interactive elements to your booth can engage customers and encourage them to spend more time exploring your products. Offering promotions, contests, or free samples are also effective ways to boost sales and create buzz around your booth.

1. **Product Demonstrations**: If your product benefits from being demonstrated (such as a cooking tool, skincare product, or art supply), set up a demonstration area where customers can see your product in action. Demonstrations not only showcase the value of your product but also give you the opportunity to engage with customers and answer any questions they may have.

2. **Samples**: Free samples are a powerful tool for attracting customers, especially if you sell food, beverages, or beauty products. Offering a small sample allows people to

experience your product firsthand, which can increase the likelihood of them making a purchase.

3. **Contests and Giveaways**: Running a contest or giveaway is a fun way to engage customers and generate excitement around your booth. For example, you could offer a prize for anyone who signs up for your email list or follows you on social media. This not only drives foot traffic to your booth but also helps you build a customer base for future marketing efforts.

Conclusion: Setting Up for Success

Creating an eye-catching vending setup is about more than just aesthetics—it's about designing a space that reflects your brand, engages customers, and makes it easy for them to purchase your products. By focusing on visual appeal, layout, branding, and interactive elements, you can create a booth that not only attracts attention but also fosters meaningful connections with customers.

In the next chapter, we will explore how to set the right price for your products and implement effective payment options that cater to a variety of customers and maximize sales opportunities.

CHAPTER 4

SETTING THE RIGHT PRICE AND PAYMENT OPTIONS

Pricing your products and providing accessible payment options are two crucial factors that can determine the success of your vending business. Setting the right price ensures that you are covering your costs, making a profit, and positioning your products competitively within the market. Meanwhile, offering convenient payment methods ensures that customers can make purchases easily, without any unnecessary friction. In this chapter, we will explore pricing strategies that can help you attract customers and maintain profitability, as well as how to choose the best payment options to streamline your vending operations.

The Importance of Setting the Right Price

Pricing your products correctly is one of the most challenging yet essential aspects of running a vending business. If your prices are too high, you risk turning potential customers away. On the other hand, if your prices are too low, you may struggle to cover your costs and undervalue your products. The goal is to find a pricing sweet spot that balances customer demand with profitability.

Here are some key reasons why setting the right price is so important:

1. **Profitability**: Your pricing must cover not only the cost of producing your products but also your operational expenses, such as booth fees, transportation, marketing, and any additional costs related to your vending business.

Setting the right price ensures that you make a profit after covering all your expenses.

2. **Perceived Value**: Pricing also plays a role in how customers perceive the value of your product. In many cases, customers associate higher prices with better quality, and if your prices are too low, they may assume your product is of inferior quality. On the flip side, if your prices are too high without justification, customers may feel they are not getting good value for their money.

3. **Market Positioning**: Your price communicates your brand's positioning in the marketplace. For example, if you are selling premium handmade goods, your price should reflect the time, effort, and craftsmanship that goes into creating your products. If you price your items too low, you may dilute your brand's premium appeal.

4. **Competitiveness**: You also need to consider how your prices compare to those of your competitors. While you don't need to match competitors' prices exactly, it's important to be aware of the pricing landscape. Pricing too far above or below the competition can influence customer decisions, so it's important to strike a balance between being competitive and maintaining your margins.

Factors to Consider When Setting Prices

When determining the right price for your products, several factors come into play. It's essential to take a holistic view of your business and market conditions to set prices that are fair, profitable, and attractive to customers. Here are some key factors to consider:

1. **Cost of Goods Sold (COGS)**: The foundation of any pricing strategy is ensuring that you cover the cost of producing your goods. This includes the direct costs of materials, labor, and manufacturing, as well as any indirect costs such

as packaging, shipping, and storage. To determine your COGS, add up all of these costs for each product, and use this as the baseline for your pricing.

2. **Operational Expenses**: In addition to your COGS, you need to account for the ongoing expenses of running your business. These expenses include booth fees, event registration, marketing, transportation, insurance, and utilities. Your pricing should be high enough to cover both your COGS and your operational expenses while still allowing room for profit.

3. **Desired Profit Margin**: Once you've calculated your costs, it's time to determine how much profit you want to make on each sale. This is where your desired profit margin comes into play. For example, if your COGS is $10 per unit and you want a 50% profit margin, you would set the price at $15. It's important to ensure that your desired profit margin is realistic and competitive within your market.

4. **Customer Perception and Willingness to Pay**: Pricing should also reflect what your target customers are willing to pay for your product. Understanding your audience's purchasing behavior, income level, and preferences will help you set prices that are both appealing and accessible. If you're selling luxury items or artisanal goods, your customers may be willing to pay a premium for quality and craftsmanship. On the other hand, if you're vending at a more budget-conscious event, you may need to adjust your prices to match the audience's expectations.

5. **Market Demand**: Market demand plays a significant role in determining price. If your product is unique or highly sought after, you may have the opportunity to charge a higher price. However, if your product is one of many

similar offerings at an event, competitive pricing may be necessary to attract customers.

6. **Seasonality and Event-Specific Pricing**: Some events may allow you to charge premium prices due to seasonal demand or the exclusivity of the venue. For example, a holiday market or a festival with limited-time vendors might justify higher pricing because customers are seeking unique gifts or experiences. Conversely, a regular farmers market or street fair may require more competitive pricing due to frequent vendor turnover and customer price sensitivity.

Pricing Strategies

Once you have a clear understanding of the factors that influence pricing, you can choose a strategy that works best for your business. Here are a few common pricing strategies for vendors:

1. **Cost-Plus Pricing**: This is a straightforward approach where you add a specific profit margin to the cost of producing the product. For example, if your COGS is $10 and you want a 40% profit margin, you would set the price at $14. This strategy ensures that you cover all costs and make a profit, but it may not take into account market demand or competition.

2. **Competitive Pricing**: With competitive pricing, you set your prices based on what similar vendors or competitors are charging. This approach helps ensure that your products are priced within a range that customers expect. However, it's important not to base your pricing solely on what competitors are doing—make sure your costs and profit margins are still covered.

3. **Value-Based Pricing**: Value-based pricing is determined by what customers perceive your product to be worth. If your

product is high-quality, unique, or offers additional benefits (such as being handmade, eco-friendly, or artisanal), customers may be willing to pay more for it. This strategy allows you to command higher prices based on the perceived value of your product rather than just the cost to produce it.

4. **Tiered Pricing**: Offering tiered pricing provides customers with different options based on their budget or preferences. For example, you could offer basic products at a lower price point and premium versions at a higher price point. This allows you to appeal to a wider range of customers without compromising on profitability.

5. **Discounts and Promotions**: Offering discounts or promotions can attract new customers or encourage existing ones to buy more. Consider offering bulk discounts, bundle deals, or seasonal promotions to drive sales. However, be careful not to discount too frequently, as this can devalue your product and reduce your overall profitability.

Choosing the Right Payment Options

In addition to setting the right price, offering a variety of payment options is essential for maximizing sales. Customers today expect flexibility and convenience when making purchases, so providing multiple payment methods ensures that you don't lose potential sales because of limited payment options. Here are some common payment methods you should consider:

1. **Cash Payments**: Cash remains a popular payment method, especially at farmers markets, festivals, and other outdoor events. Ensure that you have enough change on hand to accommodate cash transactions and consider using a secure cash box or lockable drawer to store money during

the event. Display signs indicating that you accept cash to make it clear to customers.

2. **Credit and Debit Cards**: Accepting credit and debit cards is essential for modern vendors. Many customers prefer the convenience of card payments, and some may not carry cash at all. Mobile card readers like Square, PayPal Here, and Stripe Terminal make it easy to accept card payments using your smartphone or tablet. These readers typically charge a small processing fee per transaction, so be sure to factor that into your pricing.

3. **Mobile Payment Apps**: Mobile payment apps like Apple Pay, Google Pay, and Venmo are becoming increasingly popular, particularly among younger customers. These apps allow for contactless payments, which can be especially appealing in the post-pandemic world where customers prefer minimal physical contact. Make sure you display signs indicating that you accept mobile payments to encourage customers to use these methods.

4. **Contactless Payments**: Contactless payment methods, including tap-to-pay options and QR code payments, are fast and convenient for customers. Contactless payments also reduce the need for physical interaction, making them more hygienic and efficient. Offering contactless payments can help you serve customers quickly, especially during busy events.

5. **Online Payment Links**: Some vendors offer online payment links or invoicing options, allowing customers to pay through a secure website. This can be useful for larger purchases or pre-orders where customers may prefer to pay electronically. Payment platforms like PayPal and Square offer invoicing tools that allow you to send payment links via email or text.

Streamlining the Checkout Process

Making the checkout process as smooth and simple as possible is key to ensuring customer satisfaction and increasing sales. A slow or complicated payment process can lead to frustration and missed opportunities, especially if customers are in a hurry or there's a long line at your booth. Here are some tips to streamline the checkout process:

1. **Be Prepared**: Before the event starts, ensure that all your payment systems are set up, tested, and ready to go. Have your mobile card reader charged and connected, and make sure you have plenty of cash and change on hand. The more prepared you are, the smoother the transaction process will be for your customers.

2. **Keep the Line Moving**: If you have a high volume of customers, it's important to keep the line moving quickly to avoid bottlenecks. Train your staff (if applicable) to handle transactions efficiently, and consider setting up a separate area for customers to bag their purchases or receive additional assistance after paying.

3. **Display Payment Options Clearly**: Let customers know which payment methods you accept by displaying clear signs at your booth. This will reduce confusion and help customers prepare to pay. If you accept mobile payments or contactless payments, display logos for Apple Pay, Google Pay, Venmo, or other platforms to signal that these options are available.

Conclusion: Balancing Price and Convenience for Maximum Sales

Setting the right price and offering flexible payment options are two fundamental pillars of a successful vending business. By taking the time to carefully calculate your costs, consider market demand, and factor in customer preferences, you can set prices that are both fair and profitable. Additionally, offering a variety of payment options ensures that your customers can complete their purchases easily, without any unnecessary barriers.

In the next chapter, we will explore inventory management strategies that help you stay organized, avoid overstocking or understocking, and ensure that you always have the right amount of product to meet customer demand. Proper inventory management is key to maintaining a well-run vending operation and maximizing profitability.

CHAPTER 5

INVENTORY MANAGEMENT FOR VENDING EVENTS

Managing inventory is one of the most crucial aspects of running a successful vending business. It involves understanding how much stock you need for each event, ensuring you don't overstock or understock, and maintaining control over your product offerings to maximize sales while minimizing waste. Effective inventory management can mean the difference between making a profit and losing money at vending events. In this chapter, we will explore the importance of inventory management, strategies for keeping track of your stock, and how to make informed decisions about restocking and product diversification.

The Importance of Inventory Management

Proper inventory management is essential for vending success because it directly affects your ability to meet customer demand, manage costs, and maintain profitability. Here are some key reasons why inventory management is so critical for vendors:

1. **Avoiding Stockouts**: Running out of popular products during a vending event can lead to missed sales opportunities and disappointed customers. By carefully tracking your inventory and estimating how much stock you'll need, you can avoid stockouts and ensure that you always have enough of your best-selling items on hand.

2. **Minimizing Overstock**: On the flip side, bringing too much inventory can result in unnecessary costs and wasted resources. Overstocking ties up your capital in unsold

products and can make it difficult to transport and store your goods. In the case of perishable items, overstocking can lead to spoilage, forcing you to discard products and take a loss.

3. **Improving Cash Flow**: Inventory is one of the largest expenses for most vendors, so managing it effectively can significantly impact your cash flow. By optimizing your inventory levels, you can reduce the amount of money tied up in unsold stock and ensure that you have enough cash on hand to cover other expenses like booth fees, transportation, and marketing.

4. **Understanding Customer Preferences**: Inventory management isn't just about having enough products on hand—it's also about understanding what your customers want to buy. By tracking sales data and analyzing which products sell the most, you can make informed decisions about which items to stock in the future. This helps you tailor your offerings to customer demand and maximize your sales potential.

5. **Enhancing Customer Satisfaction**: Customers expect vendors to have their products readily available. When you have a well-managed inventory, you can meet customer expectations by having popular products in stock, reducing wait times, and offering a variety of choices. This leads to higher customer satisfaction, repeat business, and positive word-of-mouth.

Estimating Demand for Each Event

One of the biggest challenges vendors face is estimating how much inventory to bring to each event. This can vary based on factors like the size of the event, the type of customers in attendance, and the length of the event. Here are some strategies to help you estimate demand and avoid the pitfalls of overstocking or understocking:

1. **Research the Event**: Before the event, gather as much information as possible about the event's expected attendance, demographics, and the types of products that typically sell well. If possible, look at past events hosted by the same organizer or attend the event as a visitor to get a sense of the crowd size and buying habits. This research can help you make informed decisions about how much stock to bring.

2. **Analyze Sales Data**: If you've vended at similar events before, review your past sales data to identify patterns. Look for trends in which products sold the most, which didn't perform as well, and how much stock you sold overall. Use this data to inform your stocking decisions for future events. For example, if you notice that you consistently sell out of a particular product, consider bringing more of it to the next event.

3. **Consider Event Size and Duration**: The size and duration of the event are important factors in estimating demand. A large, multi-day event will likely require more inventory than a small, one-day event. Additionally, events with high foot traffic, such as festivals or trade shows, may result in more sales opportunities, so you'll need to adjust your inventory accordingly.

4. **Monitor Seasonal Trends**: Seasonality can play a big role in customer demand, especially if your products are tied to specific holidays or seasonal activities. For example, if you sell holiday-themed items, you'll likely see a spike in demand during the holiday season. Pay attention to these seasonal trends and adjust your inventory levels to match customer preferences during different times of the year.

5. **Factor in Lead Time**: If you produce your own products, consider the lead time required to restock inventory. For example, if your items are handmade and take time to produce, you may need to plan your inventory levels well in advance of the event. Make sure you have enough stock to meet demand without running into production delays.

Keeping Track of Inventory

Once you've estimated how much stock to bring to an event, the next step is keeping track of your inventory before, during, and after the event. Accurate inventory tracking helps you stay organized, avoid stockouts, and make better decisions about restocking. Here are some methods for tracking your inventory:

1. **Manual Inventory Tracking**: If you're a small vendor with a limited product range, manual tracking may be sufficient. This involves keeping a written record of how much inventory you have before the event, noting sales during the event, and recording what's left afterward. While this method is straightforward, it can be time-consuming and prone to errors if you have a large inventory or multiple product categories.

2. **Spreadsheet Tracking**: Using a spreadsheet to track your inventory is a step up from manual tracking and offers more flexibility. With a spreadsheet, you can create columns for each product, track the starting inventory, sales during the event, and the remaining stock. Spreadsheets allow you to quickly calculate how much stock you've sold and how much you need to reorder.

3. **Inventory Management Software**: As your vending business grows, you may want to invest in inventory management software that automates the tracking process. These tools allow you to track your inventory in real-time, manage

multiple product categories, and generate reports on sales and stock levels. Popular inventory management tools like Square, Shopify, and Vend offer features that integrate with your payment systems, making it easier to manage inventory while processing sales.

4. **Mobile Apps**: Mobile apps can also be a convenient way to track inventory, especially if you're on the go. Apps like Sortly, Inventory Now, and Stock Control offer easy-to-use inventory management solutions that allow you to scan barcodes, track stock levels, and manage your inventory directly from your smartphone or tablet.

5. **Regular Stock Audits**: Regardless of which method you use to track inventory, it's important to conduct regular stock audits. Before each event, take an inventory of your stock to ensure you have accurate records. After the event, conduct another audit to compare your starting inventory with the sales you made. This helps you identify any discrepancies and ensures that your inventory records are up to date.

Restocking and Product Diversification

Effective inventory management also involves knowing when to restock and how to diversify your product offerings. Here are some tips for managing restocking and product diversification:

1. **Restock Popular Items**: Pay close attention to which products consistently sell well and make sure to restock them for future events. It's better to have an abundance of popular items that you know will sell than to bring a variety of less popular items that may sit on the shelf. However, be careful not to overstock on a single item—always consider event-specific demand and trends.

2. **Introduce New Products Gradually**: While it's important to restock popular items, introducing new products can also help you keep your offerings fresh and attract repeat customers. Consider testing new products or variations of existing products at smaller events before bringing them to larger markets. This allows you to gauge customer interest and avoid over-investing in new inventory before knowing how well it will sell.

3. **Seasonal Adjustments**: Make seasonal adjustments to your inventory based on the time of year and the type of event. For example, if you sell clothing, you may want to bring lighter fabrics and designs in the summer and heavier, cozier options in the winter. Similarly, if you sell food products, consider offering seasonal flavors or limited-edition items that align with the time of year or special holidays.

4. **Monitor Slow-Moving Products**: Not all products will sell as quickly as others. If you notice that certain items are moving slowly, consider offering them at a discount or bundling them with other products to clear out your inventory. This can help free up space and capital for new products that have a higher likelihood of selling.

5. **Stay Flexible**: Flexibility is key to successful inventory management. Be willing to adjust your product offerings, restocking schedules, and inventory levels based on customer demand, event size, and sales trends. By staying flexible and adaptable, you can ensure that your vending business remains profitable and responsive to market conditions.

Conclusion: Mastering Inventory for Vending Success

Effective inventory management is a cornerstone of a successful vending business. By accurately estimating demand, keeping track of your stock, and making informed decisions about restocking and product diversification, you can ensure that you always have the right products on hand to meet customer demand. Inventory management not only helps you maximize sales but also ensures that you're managing costs and maintaining profitability.

In the next chapter, we will explore customer engagement strategies to help you draw people to your booth, connect with potential buyers, and ultimately drive more sales. Customer interaction is a key factor in building relationships and ensuring repeat business, and we'll cover the best practices for engaging customers at vending events.

CHAPTER 6

ENGAGING CUSTOMERS AND DRIVING SALES

One of the most critical aspects of vending success is your ability to engage customers effectively. Attracting people to your booth, making meaningful connections, and driving sales requires more than just having a well-stocked inventory or an attractive setup. It's about creating a welcoming atmosphere, understanding customer psychology, and utilizing effective sales techniques. In this chapter, we will explore proven strategies for engaging customers, building rapport, and converting foot traffic into paying customers. We'll also look at how to cultivate repeat business, turning one-time buyers into loyal supporters.

The Importance of Customer Engagement

Customer engagement is the foundation of successful vending. It refers to the way you interact with potential buyers, making them feel welcomed, valued, and informed. Engaged customers are more likely to stop by your booth, explore your products, and make a purchase. Beyond that, strong engagement can lead to lasting relationships that result in repeat business and word-of-mouth referrals.

Here's why customer engagement is so crucial:

1. **First Impressions Matter**: How you greet and approach customers can set the tone for their entire shopping experience. A positive, friendly first impression can encourage people to linger and browse your products,

while a lack of engagement may cause them to walk by without giving your booth a second glance.

2. **Building Trust**: Personal interaction helps build trust with potential buyers. People are more likely to purchase from vendors they feel comfortable with, especially if they are unfamiliar with the product or brand. Trust-building through genuine engagement can turn hesitant browsers into confident buyers.

3. **Understanding Customer Needs**: Engaging with customers allows you to better understand their needs, preferences, and concerns. This information can help you tailor your sales pitch and recommend products that align with their desires, increasing the likelihood of making a sale.

4. **Creating Memorable Experiences**: Customer engagement isn't just about making a sale—it's about creating a memorable experience. When customers feel valued and appreciated, they are more likely to remember your booth and brand, even after the event is over. This can lead to repeat business and positive word-of-mouth.

Approaching Customers: The Art of the Greeting

The way you greet potential customers can make or break their decision to stop at your booth. A warm, approachable greeting sets a positive tone and invites customers to engage with you. Here are some tips for crafting the perfect greeting:

1. **Be Friendly and Approachable**: Smile and make eye contact with customers as they approach your booth. A genuine, friendly demeanor signals that you're approachable and ready to help. Avoid sitting behind your booth with a phone or looking disengaged, as this can make customers feel unwelcome.

2. **Keep It Casual**: Your greeting doesn't need to be overly formal or salesy. A simple "Hi, how are you?" or "Let me know if you have any questions" is often enough to open the door to further conversation. Avoid launching straight into a sales pitch, as this can feel pushy and off-putting.

3. **Gauge Customer Interest**: Not every customer will want to engage right away, and that's okay. Give them space to browse if they prefer, but remain available to answer questions or offer assistance. Respecting a customer's need for space can actually increase their comfort and make them more likely to approach you when they're ready.

4. **Offer a Compliment or Observation**: Sometimes, a compliment or observation can help break the ice and start a conversation. For example, you might say, "I love your scarf—where did you get it?" or "This is such a great event, don't you think?" These types of comments are non-salesy and create a natural opening for dialogue.

Engaging with Customers: Active Listening and Responding

Once you've drawn a customer into your booth, the next step is to engage them in meaningful conversation. This requires active listening and thoughtful responses that build rapport and address their needs. Here's how to do it effectively:

1. **Ask Open-Ended Questions**: Instead of asking yes-or-no questions, try to ask open-ended questions that encourage customers to share more about their preferences or needs. For example, "What kind of products are you looking for today?" or "Have you ever tried something like this before?" These types of questions provide valuable insights and help guide your conversation.

2. **Listen Attentively**: Pay close attention to what the customer says and avoid interrupting. Active listening shows that you value their input and are genuinely interested in helping them find what they're looking for. Nodding or using short affirmations like "I see" or "That makes sense" helps keep the conversation flowing.

3. **Tailor Your Responses**: Once you understand the customer's needs or preferences, tailor your response to address their specific situation. For example, if a customer mentions they are looking for a gift, you might recommend a popular product or share ideas for pairing items together. Personalizing your responses based on what the customer has shared increases the likelihood of making a sale.

4. **Handle Objections Gracefully**: Customers may express concerns or objections, such as price, quality, or uncertainty about the product's usefulness. Instead of getting defensive, acknowledge their concern and provide helpful information. For example, if a customer mentions that a product is too expensive, you might explain its unique value, durability, or craftsmanship. By addressing objections in a calm and informative manner, you can help alleviate doubts and build trust.

Creating an Inviting Booth Atmosphere

Beyond conversation, the atmosphere of your booth plays a key role in engaging customers. A welcoming, organized space encourages customers to explore your products and stay longer, increasing the chances of making a sale. Here are some ways to create an inviting booth atmosphere:

1. **Maintain a Clean and Organized Display**: Clutter can overwhelm customers and make it difficult for them to focus on your products. Keep your booth clean, organized,

and visually appealing. Use shelves, racks, and tables to display products at different heights and create clear pathways for customers to move through the space.

2. **Encourage Interaction with Products**: Encourage customers to touch, try, or sample your products whenever possible. For example, if you sell handmade jewelry, place pieces within easy reach so customers can pick them up and try them on. If you sell food or beverages, offer free samples to entice customers to taste before they buy. Engaging the senses can create a more immersive shopping experience and increase the likelihood of a purchase.

3. **Offer Clear Signage**: Customers appreciate clear and easy-to-read signage that provides product information, pricing, and any special promotions. Display your signage prominently so that customers can easily understand what you're offering without needing to ask. This helps them feel more confident in their decision-making process.

4. **Use Friendly Body Language**: Your body language can communicate a lot about how approachable and engaged you are. Stand or sit upright, smile, and avoid crossing your arms, which can create a barrier between you and the customer. Be ready to move around your booth to assist customers or demonstrate products.

Sales Techniques: Converting Browsers into Buyers

Once you've successfully engaged a customer, the next step is to guide them toward making a purchase. This requires tact, persuasion, and a focus on providing value without being overly pushy. Here are some effective sales techniques for vendors:

1. **Highlight Benefits, Not Just Features**: Customers don't just want to know what your product does—they want to know how it will benefit them. Focus on the value your product

provides, whether it's its functionality, uniqueness, quality, or how it solves a problem. For example, instead of just saying, "This candle is handmade," you might say, "This candle is handmade using eco-friendly materials, and it burns longer than typical store-bought candles, making it a great value for your home."

2. **Create Urgency**: Creating a sense of urgency can encourage customers to act quickly rather than walk away and think about it. Limited-time offers, special discounts, or promoting the fact that you only have a few items left in stock can push customers to make a purchase on the spot. For example, "This is the last one in this color, and they've been selling fast!" can motivate a customer to act.

3. **Upsell and Cross-Sell**: Upselling involves encouraging customers to purchase a higher-end version of a product, while cross-selling suggests complementary products that enhance the original purchase. For example, if a customer is buying a bracelet, you might suggest a matching necklace or earrings to complete the look. Upselling and cross-selling can increase your average transaction size and provide customers with a better overall experience.

4. **Close the Sale with Confidence**: Once a customer seems ready to buy, confidently guide them through the purchasing process. You can say something like, "I'm so glad you love this! Let me wrap it up for you." By assuming the sale and moving forward with closing, you make it easier for the customer to commit.

Building Relationships for Repeat Business

One of the most valuable aspects of vending is the opportunity to build relationships with customers that lead to repeat business. Here are some ways to foster long-term connections:

1. **Collect Customer Information**: If possible, collect customer email addresses or follow them on social media. This allows you to stay in touch after the event and inform them of future vending dates, new products, or special offers.

2. **Provide a Memorable Experience**: Go the extra mile to create a positive, memorable experience for your customers. Whether it's offering personalized recommendations, packaging their purchase beautifully, or including a thank-you note, small touches can make a big impression.

3. **Follow Up After the Event**: After the event, consider sending a follow-up email to thank your customers for visiting your booth and encourage them to shop with you again, either at future events or online.

Conclusion: Engaging Customers for Lasting Success

Engaging customers is not just about making sales—it's about building connections, creating memorable experiences, and fostering long-term relationships that lead to repeat business. By approaching customers with warmth, listening to their needs, and using thoughtful sales techniques, you can turn casual browsers into loyal customers. A customer-focused approach will set your vending business apart, helping you build a positive reputation and ensuring lasting success.

In the next chapter, we will explore how to navigate competition at vending events, helping you differentiate yourself from other vendors and position your booth as the go-to destination for customers.

CHAPTER 7

NAVIGATING COMPETITION AT VENDING EVENTS

Vending events often feature a wide range of vendors, all competing for the attention of attendees. Whether you're at a local farmers market, a craft fair, or a large festival, there will likely be other vendors selling similar products or vying for the same customer base. Navigating competition effectively is essential for standing out, attracting customers, and ultimately succeeding in a crowded market. In this chapter, we'll explore strategies to differentiate yourself from other vendors, highlight your unique selling points, and foster a positive attitude toward competition.

Understanding Competition and Its Impact on Vending Success

Competition at vending events can feel overwhelming, but it's also a normal part of running a business. While it might seem like your competitors are your biggest obstacle, the reality is that competition often drives innovation and pushes you to improve your offerings, presentation, and overall approach to selling. Instead of viewing competition as a threat, think of it as an opportunity to learn, grow, and refine your vending strategy.

Here's how competition can impact your vending business:

1. **Customer Choice**: With so many vendors offering similar products, customers have more options to choose from. This means that your product needs to stand out, whether through its quality, pricing, presentation, or the customer experience you provide.

2. **Price Sensitivity**: Customers may compare prices between vendors selling similar products. If your pricing is significantly higher than your competitors, you may struggle to make sales unless you can clearly communicate why your product is worth the extra cost.

3. **Brand Differentiation**: Competition forces you to think about what makes your brand unique. Why should customers choose your booth over another vendor selling similar items? Successfully navigating competition requires a clear understanding of what sets you apart from the rest.

4. **Learning Opportunities**: Competition can also serve as a valuable learning experience. By observing other vendors, you can gain insights into what works and what doesn't, whether it's related to booth setup, customer engagement, pricing strategies, or product offerings. Competitors can teach you valuable lessons that can help you improve your own business.

Differentiating Your Booth and Products

One of the most effective ways to navigate competition at vending events is to differentiate your booth and products from other vendors. By offering something unique or creating a memorable shopping experience, you can attract customers who might otherwise be drawn to a competitor's booth.

Here are several strategies for differentiating yourself from the competition:

1. **Unique Product Offerings**: The most straightforward way to stand out is by offering products that are distinct from what other vendors are selling. If you sell handcrafted items, consider offering custom-made products or limited-edition collections that aren't available anywhere else. If you sell food or beverages, experiment with

unique flavors or ingredients that set you apart from other vendors.

2. **Quality and Craftsmanship**: If your products are priced higher than your competitors, make sure that customers understand why. Emphasize the quality and craftsmanship that goes into making your products. For example, if you use premium materials or sustainable practices, share this information with customers. High-quality products, especially those that are handmade or locally sourced, can justify a higher price point and appeal to customers who value authenticity.

3. **Packaging and Presentation**: The way you present your products can make a significant difference in how customers perceive them. Eye-catching packaging, thoughtful presentation, and attention to detail can elevate your products and create a more premium experience. If two vendors are selling similar products, but your booth has beautifully packaged items and a more organized display, customers are likely to gravitate toward your booth.

4. **Booth Design and Atmosphere**: A well-designed booth can help you stand out in a sea of vendors. Pay attention to your booth's layout, signage, and overall aesthetic. Create a cohesive and visually appealing space that reflects your brand's personality. Consider adding special touches like string lights, banners, or unique signage that make your booth more inviting and memorable.

5. **Customer Experience**: Beyond the products themselves, the experience you provide to customers can set you apart from the competition. Offering exceptional customer service, engaging with customers in a friendly and genuine manner, and creating a welcoming atmosphere at your

booth can make a lasting impression. Customers are more likely to remember and return to vendors who make them feel valued and appreciated.

Pricing Strategies to Compete Effectively

Pricing plays a key role in how you compete with other vendors. Customers often compare prices between similar products, so it's important to consider how your pricing aligns with the competition and whether it reflects the value you offer.

Here are some pricing strategies to help you compete effectively:

1. **Value-Based Pricing**: Rather than pricing your products solely based on cost, consider using a value-based pricing approach. This means setting prices based on the perceived value of your product to the customer. If your product offers unique benefits, such as being handcrafted, eco-friendly, or made with premium materials, you can justify a higher price by highlighting these aspects.

2. **Competitive Pricing**: If you're competing with vendors who offer similar products, you may need to price your items competitively to attract customers. Research what your competitors are charging and adjust your pricing accordingly. However, be cautious about underpricing your products, as this can devalue your brand and make it difficult to maintain profitability.

3. **Bundle Deals and Discounts**: Offering bundle deals or discounts can be an effective way to attract customers and stand out from the competition. For example, you could offer a discount for purchasing multiple items or create a gift set that combines complementary products at a special price. Bundle deals not only increase the average transaction size but also create a sense of value for the customer.

4. **Promotions and Limited-Time Offers**: Running promotions or limited-time offers can create a sense of urgency and encourage customers to buy from you rather than a competitor. For example, you might offer a 10% discount for purchases made before noon or a free gift with purchases over a certain amount. Promotions can help you differentiate yourself from competitors and drive sales during the event.

Building Relationships with Competitors

While it may seem counterintuitive, building relationships with your competitors can actually benefit your vending business. Networking with other vendors fosters a sense of community and opens up opportunities for collaboration, referrals, and shared learning.

Here's how building positive relationships with competitors can help you succeed:

1. **Collaboration Opportunities**: Working with other vendors opens the door to potential collaborations, such as creating joint promotions or hosting pop-up events together. For example, if you sell handmade soaps and a neighboring vendor sells bath accessories, you could collaborate on a bundled gift set that combines both of your products.

2. **Referrals**: Building rapport with other vendors can lead to referrals. If a customer is looking for something specific that you don't offer, referring them to a competitor (and vice versa) can foster goodwill and create opportunities for future collaborations. Additionally, competitors may refer customers to you if they're overbooked or don't have the inventory to meet demand.

3. **Shared Insights and Knowledge**: Competitors can be valuable sources of insight and knowledge. By networking with other vendors, you can share tips on what works and

what doesn't, from booth setup to customer engagement strategies. Learning from others' experiences can help you refine your own approach and avoid common pitfalls.

4. **Supporting the Community**: By fostering a sense of community among vendors, you create a positive environment where everyone benefits. Supporting each other through encouragement and shared resources can help everyone succeed in a competitive market. In the long run, a strong vendor community can attract more customers to events and create a more vibrant marketplace.

Handling Competitive Pressure with Confidence

Navigating competition at vending events can be stressful, especially if you feel like you're constantly comparing yourself to other vendors. However, it's important to handle competitive pressure with confidence and focus on what you do best.

Here are some strategies for maintaining confidence in a competitive environment:

1. **Focus on Your Strengths**: Rather than worrying about what your competitors are doing, focus on your own strengths and what makes your brand unique. Highlight the aspects of your business that set you apart, whether it's the quality of your products, the customer experience you provide, or your personal story as a vendor.

2. **Stay Adaptable**: Flexibility is key to succeeding in a competitive market. Be willing to adapt your approach based on customer feedback, market trends, and event dynamics. If you notice that a particular product isn't selling as well as expected, be prepared to pivot and focus on other items that are more popular.

3. **Manage Your Expectations**: It's natural to feel disappointed if your sales don't meet your expectations, especially when facing tough competition. However, it's important to keep perspective and recognize that not every event will be a home run. Use each event as a learning experience and focus on building long-term success rather than getting discouraged by short-term setbacks.

4. **Celebrate Small Wins**: In a competitive environment, even small victories are worth celebrating. Whether it's making a new connection, selling out of a popular product, or receiving positive feedback from a customer, take time to acknowledge your achievements and build on them for future success.

Conclusion: Thriving in a Competitive Environment

Competition is an inevitable part of vending, but it doesn't have to be a barrier to success. By focusing on what makes your brand and products unique, pricing your items strategically, and fostering positive relationships with other vendors, you can navigate competition with confidence and turn challenges into opportunities. Remember that competition drives innovation, and by continually improving your offerings and customer experience, you can stand out in even the most crowded markets.

In the next chapter, we will explore marketing strategies that can help you promote your vending business before, during, and after events, ensuring that you reach a wider audience and attract more customers to your booth. Marketing is a powerful tool for building awareness, driving traffic, and increasing sales, both online and offline.

CHAPTER 8

MARKETING BEFORE, DURING, AND AFTER VENDING EVENTS

Marketing is a crucial aspect of running a successful vending business. While your booth setup, customer engagement, and product quality are important, they are only part of the equation. To truly maximize your vending opportunities, you need to create buzz around your business and attract customers both before, during, and after vending events. In this chapter, we'll dive into effective marketing strategies that will help you stand out, build brand recognition, and increase sales.

The Importance of Marketing for Vending Success

Vending events are competitive spaces, often featuring dozens or even hundreds of vendors. Without a strong marketing strategy, it's easy to get lost in the crowd. Marketing allows you to differentiate yourself from competitors, build excitement around your products, and attract a steady stream of customers to your booth.

Effective marketing goes beyond just announcing your participation in an event. It involves creating a consistent and memorable brand presence that engages customers and keeps them coming back for more. Whether you're leveraging social media, email marketing, or in-person promotional tactics, marketing should be an ongoing effort before, during, and after the event.

Marketing Before the Event

Your marketing efforts should begin well before the event date. Building anticipation and informing potential customers about your participation is key to ensuring that you have a strong turnout at your booth. Here are several pre-event marketing strategies to help you create buzz:

1. Social Media Promotion

Social media platforms like Instagram, Facebook, and Twitter are invaluable tools for promoting your vending business and connecting with your audience. Start by creating posts that announce your participation in the event, using engaging visuals and clear information about the time, location, and what you'll be offering.

- **Instagram and Facebook Stories**: Utilize Instagram and Facebook Stories to give behind-the-scenes peeks of your event preparation. This could include sneak peeks of the products you'll be selling, shots of your booth setup, or even videos of you crafting your goods. Stories are a great way to build excitement and give your audience a personal look at your business.

- **Countdowns and Reminders**: Use social media tools like countdown stickers or event reminders to create a sense of urgency and anticipation. Encourage your followers to mark their calendars and attend the event.

- **Hashtags and Geotags**: Research relevant hashtags for the event, your products, and your local area. Using event-specific hashtags helps you reach attendees who are already interested in the event. Additionally, geotagging your posts with the event location can increase your visibility to local customers.

2. Email Marketing

If you have an email list of past customers or followers, use it to send targeted promotions leading up to the event. Email marketing allows for more personalized communication and can help remind your audience to visit your booth. Here's how you can leverage email marketing before an event:

- **Announcement Emails**: Send out an email announcing your participation in the upcoming event. Include details like the event name, location, dates, and any special promotions you'll be offering. Highlight what makes your products unique and why customers should visit your booth.

- **Exclusive Offers**: Consider offering a special discount or exclusive deal to your email subscribers if they visit your booth at the event. This not only incentivizes them to attend but also builds loyalty by rewarding your existing customer base.

3. Collaborate with Event Organizers

Many event organizers have their own marketing channels, including social media, email newsletters, and websites. Reach out to the event organizers to see if they offer vendor spotlights, features, or opportunities to promote your business through their platforms. Being featured by the event itself can significantly boost your visibility and attract more attendees to your booth.

4. Flyers and Posters

For local events, printed materials like flyers and posters can still be an effective marketing tool, especially if you're targeting a local audience. Distribute flyers at nearby businesses, cafes, or community centers that align with your target demographic. Including a coupon or a special offer on the flyer can further incentivize people to visit your booth.

Marketing During the Event

Once the event begins, your marketing efforts don't stop. In fact, marketing during the event is just as important as your pre-event promotions. Your goal is to capture the attention of attendees and create an engaging experience that encourages them to stop by your booth, explore your products, and make a purchase.

1. Live Social Media Coverage

Live social media coverage during the event is an excellent way to engage both event attendees and your online audience. Posting live updates, stories, and videos from the event gives your followers a sense of immediacy and excitement.

- **Instagram Live or Facebook Live**: Consider going live on Instagram or Facebook to showcase your booth setup, demonstrate your products, or share the energy of the event. Encourage attendees to visit your booth in person by mentioning any exclusive offers or promotions.

- **Real-Time Stories**: Post regular updates to your Instagram or Facebook Stories throughout the day. Include photos or videos of happy customers, product demonstrations, and the overall vibe of the event. Don't forget to use relevant hashtags, geotags, and event-specific tags to maximize visibility.

2. In-Booth Promotions and Giveaways

Creating an interactive and engaging experience at your booth is key to attracting and retaining customers during the event. One effective way to drive foot traffic is by offering in-booth promotions or giveaways.

- **Offer Discounts or Bundles**: Consider offering event-exclusive discounts or bundle deals to encourage purchases. For example, offer a 10% discount on purchases over a certain amount, or bundle complementary products together at a reduced price.

- **Free Samples**: If your products lend themselves to sampling (e.g., food, cosmetics, or candles), offer free samples to passersby. Free samples allow customers to experience your product firsthand, making them more likely to make a purchase.

- **Giveaways and Contests**: Host a giveaway or contest that attendees can enter by providing their email address or following you on social media. This not only attracts people to your booth but also helps you build your email list or social media following for future marketing efforts.

3. Capture Customer Information

While your primary goal during the event is to make sales, it's also important to think long-term. Capturing customer information, such as email addresses or social media handles, allows you to stay in touch with them after the event and encourage repeat business.

- **Email Sign-Up List**: Offer a small incentive for customers who sign up for your email list, such as a discount on their next purchase or a free gift. This helps you grow your customer database and stay connected with people after the event.

- **QR Codes**: Use QR codes to make it easy for customers to follow you on social media or visit your website. Display the QR code prominently at your booth, and consider offering a small discount for customers who follow you on the spot.

Marketing After the Event

The event may be over, but your marketing efforts shouldn't end there. Following up with customers and maintaining a connection after the event is key to building lasting relationships and encouraging repeat business. Here are some post-event marketing strategies to keep the momentum going:

1. Post-Event Thank You and Follow-Up Emails

Send a thank-you email to customers who visited your booth and made a purchase, as well as those who signed up for your email list. Express your appreciation for their support, and include a special discount or offer to encourage them to make a future purchase, either online or at your next event.

- **Exclusive Offers for Email Subscribers**: Consider offering an exclusive discount or free shipping on their next purchase as a token of appreciation for visiting your booth. This not only encourages repeat business but also reinforces the value of being on your email list.

2. Share Event Highlights on Social Media

Share highlights from the event on your social media channels to keep the conversation going. Post photos of happy customers, snapshots of your booth, and behind-the-scenes moments from the event. This content serves as a reminder of your brand and helps keep you top-of-mind for followers who may not have attended the event but are interested in your products.

3. Customer Testimonials and Reviews

If you received positive feedback from customers during the event, ask them to leave a review on your website, social media, or review platforms like Google or Yelp. Positive reviews and testimonials can boost your credibility and attract new customers in the future. You can also share customer testimonials on your social media accounts to build trust with your audience.

4. Prepare for the Next Event

Use the insights gained from the event to refine your marketing strategies for future events. Analyze what worked well, what didn't, and how you can improve. Continue building relationships with customers and event organizers to ensure you're ready for the next vending opportunity.

Conclusion: A Holistic Approach to Vending Marketing

Effective marketing is essential for building your brand, attracting customers, and driving sales at vending events. By implementing a holistic marketing strategy that covers pre-event promotion, in-event engagement, and post-event follow-up, you can create a memorable and engaging experience that resonates with your audience.

In the next chapter, we will explore how to handle challenges and setbacks that may arise during vending events, from dealing with bad weather to navigating low foot traffic, and how to turn these obstacles into opportunities for growth.

CHAPTER 9

HANDLING CHALLENGES AND SETBACKS

Vending events can be unpredictable, and despite your best efforts, challenges and setbacks are inevitable. Whether it's bad weather, low foot traffic, unexpected competition, or logistical issues, successful vendors must be adaptable, resourceful, and resilient. Learning how to manage these obstacles effectively can make the difference between a profitable event and a frustrating experience. In this chapter, we will explore common challenges that vendors face and provide practical strategies for overcoming them, allowing you to turn setbacks into opportunities for growth and improvement.

1. Navigating Bad Weather

One of the most common challenges for vendors, especially at outdoor events, is dealing with bad weather. Rain, extreme heat, strong winds, or unexpected cold can significantly impact foot traffic and sales, and if you're not prepared, it can ruin your booth setup or damage your products.

Here are some strategies to handle weather-related challenges:

Preparation is Key

- **Check the Forecast**: In the days leading up to the event, monitor the weather forecast closely. Knowing what to expect allows you to prepare in advance by packing the necessary equipment and clothing.

- **Invest in Proper Gear**: Make sure you have the right gear to protect your booth and products. If you're vending at outdoor events, a sturdy pop-up canopy or tent is essential to shield you from the elements. Additionally, consider bringing sidewalls for your tent to protect your booth from wind and rain.

- **Protect Your Products**: Bring plastic coverings or tarps to cover your products in case of rain. If you're selling items that are particularly sensitive to moisture (e.g., clothing, paper goods, or food), store them in waterproof containers or under your table to keep them dry.

Weather-Responsive Adjustments

- **Adapt Your Booth Layout**: If heavy rain or strong winds are forecasted, adjust your booth layout accordingly. Secure any lightweight or fragile items that could blow away, and use weights to stabilize your tent or signage. Be flexible with your display setup to ensure that your products remain safe and visible, even in challenging weather.

- **Engage with Fewer Customers**: If the weather keeps people from attending the event in large numbers, you may experience fewer customers. Take advantage of the quieter atmosphere by engaging more deeply with the customers who do visit your booth. Use this time to build stronger relationships with those customers, as they're more likely to remember your personal touch and return for future events or purchases.

Weather-Specific Promotions

- **Offer Weather-Related Discounts**: If the weather is causing a slowdown in traffic, consider offering special "bad weather" discounts or promotions. Customers who brave the elements to visit the event may appreciate a good deal, which could encourage them to make a purchase they wouldn't otherwise have considered.

- **Leverage Social Media**: Use social media to let your followers know that you're still at the event, even if the weather isn't ideal. Post updates with images of your booth and any weather-related discounts you're offering. This can motivate people to come out despite the weather or remind them to visit your online store if they can't attend in person.

2. Managing Low Foot Traffic

Low foot traffic is another common issue that vendors face, especially at smaller events or during certain hours of the day. When fewer people are attending the event, it can feel discouraging, but there are several strategies you can use to make the most of slow periods.

Maximize Every Opportunity

- **Engage Every Passerby**: In events with low foot traffic, every potential customer counts. Greet every person who passes by with a friendly, non-pushy greeting. Even if they don't stop to buy, engaging with people in a positive way leaves a lasting impression, which can lead to future sales or referrals.

- **Create a Reason to Stop**: If foot traffic is slow, give people a reason to stop by your booth. This could be a fun promotion, free samples, or a contest they can enter by providing their email address. Anything that sparks curiosity can help you draw people in, even if they weren't planning to make a purchase.

Adjust Expectations

- **Track Sales Data**: Not every event will have the same level of traffic, so it's important to adjust your expectations based on the type of event you're attending. Smaller, local events may not draw the same crowds as larger festivals, but they can still provide valuable opportunities to build relationships and connect with loyal customers. Keep track of your sales data for each event to identify trends and determine what types of events are most successful for your business.

Optimize Slow Periods

- **Use Downtime for Networking**: During slow periods, take the opportunity to network with other vendors. Building relationships with fellow vendors can lead to future collaborations, referrals, or shared knowledge about successful strategies. Additionally, other vendors may provide insights into how they handle challenges like low traffic or slow sales.

- **Work on Your Business**: Slow periods at an event don't have to be wasted time. Use this time to review your inventory, reorganize your booth, or work on marketing materials like social media posts or email newsletters. By staying productive, you can use the downtime to improve your business and prepare for future events.

3. Dealing with Unexpected Competition

Vending events often feature multiple vendors selling similar products, which can create unexpected competition. While competition is a normal part of vending, it can be discouraging if a neighboring vendor is selling the same items at a lower price or has a larger, flashier booth.

Here's how to handle unexpected competition without feeling overwhelmed:

Focus on Your Strengths

- **Differentiate Yourself**: The key to navigating competition is differentiation. Focus on what makes your brand unique, whether it's the quality of your products, the personal story behind your business, or the exceptional customer service you provide. Highlight these unique selling points in your conversations with customers to help them see why your products are special.

- **Offer Customization**: One way to stand out in a crowded market is to offer customization or personalization options that your competitors may not have. For example, if you sell jewelry, you could offer on-the-spot engraving or custom color combinations. Customization adds value and gives customers a reason to choose your booth over others.

Stay Positive and Collaborative

- **Collaborate with Competitors**: Instead of seeing other vendors as a threat, consider them potential collaborators. For example, if you sell handmade candles and a neighboring vendor sells decorative candleholders, you could cross-promote each other's products or offer a bundled deal. Collaborating with other vendors creates a win-win situation and fosters a positive atmosphere.

- **Don't Engage in Price Wars**: It can be tempting to lower your prices in response to competitors who are selling similar products for less, but this strategy can devalue your brand and hurt your profitability. Instead, focus on the value you offer and educate customers about why your products are worth the price. Communicate the quality, craftsmanship, or unique features that justify your pricing.

4. Overcoming Logistical and Operational Issues

Running a vending booth involves a lot of logistics, from transportation and setup to managing your inventory and processing payments. Sometimes, things don't go as planned—your tent might break, your card reader might malfunction, or you might forget essential supplies.

Here's how to overcome these operational setbacks:

Be Prepared with Backup Plans

- **Create a Checklist**: Before every event, create a detailed checklist of everything you need to bring, from inventory to booth supplies. Having a checklist reduces the likelihood of forgetting important items like signage, display materials, or extra stock.

- **Bring Backup Equipment**: It's always a good idea to bring backup equipment in case something goes wrong. For example, if you use a card reader for payments, bring a backup device or be prepared to accept cash if your primary system fails. Similarly, if you have fragile display items like tents or shelves, pack extra parts or tools for quick repairs.

Adapt to the Unexpected

- **Stay Calm Under Pressure**: When things go wrong, staying calm and composed is essential. Take a moment to assess the situation and think through possible solutions. Often, the way you handle a problem can turn it into an opportunity to demonstrate resilience and professionalism to customers.

- **Ask for Help**: If you encounter a logistical challenge that you can't solve on your own, don't hesitate to ask for help. Event staff, fellow vendors, or even customers may be willing to assist with a quick fix or offer advice. Many vendors have encountered similar challenges and may have tips on how to resolve them efficiently.

Conclusion: Turning Setbacks Into Opportunities

Challenges and setbacks are an inevitable part of vending, but with the right mindset and strategies, you can turn these obstacles into opportunities for growth. Whether you're dealing with bad weather, low foot traffic, unexpected competition, or logistical issues, the key is to stay flexible, adaptable, and solution-oriented. By learning to navigate these challenges with confidence, you'll be better equipped to succeed in future vending events, building resilience and a reputation for professionalism along the way.

In the next chapter, we'll explore how to scale your vending business and take it to the next level, including expanding to new locations, increasing your product offerings, and leveraging online platforms to grow your customer base.

CHAPTER 10

SCALING YOUR VENDING BUSINESS

Once you've established a strong foundation for your vending business, the next logical step is to scale and grow. Scaling a business means expanding its reach, increasing revenue, and potentially exploring new opportunities beyond the traditional vending events. Whether you aim to attend larger events, diversify your product offerings, or branch out into e-commerce, scaling your vending business requires strategic planning and a clear vision for growth.

In this chapter, we'll explore the steps to successfully scale your vending business, covering key topics such as expanding to new locations, increasing your product line, leveraging online platforms, and managing operational challenges that come with growth.

1. Expanding to New Locations and Events

A natural way to scale your vending business is to attend more events or expand into new markets. This could mean exploring larger or higher-profile events, traveling to different regions, or vending at specialized events that cater to niche markets.

Research New Event Opportunities

- **Attend Larger Events**: If you've been vending at smaller, local markets, consider stepping up to larger events like regional fairs, festivals, or trade shows. These events typically attract more foot traffic and offer greater sales potential, but they also come with higher booth fees and increased competition. It's essential to research the event thoroughly, considering the target audience, booth costs, and the overall vibe of the event.

- **Diversify Event Types**: Expanding into different types of vending opportunities can also help scale your business. For example, if you usually vend at craft fairs, you might want to explore food festivals, flea markets, or corporate events. Each event type attracts a different demographic, and expanding into various markets allows you to tap into new customer bases.

Build Relationships with Event Organizers

- **Consistent Presence**: Becoming a regular at high-profile events can help you build a reputation and increase brand recognition. Many events prioritize vendors who have attended previous years, so staying in contact with organizers and securing your spot early can be beneficial.

- **Sponsorship Opportunities**: As you scale, consider partnering with event organizers through sponsorships. Sponsorship opportunities can provide additional exposure, such as your brand being featured in event marketing materials or securing a prime location at the event.

2. Expanding Your Product Line

Diversifying your product offerings is another way to scale your vending business. Expanding your product line not only increases the variety you offer but also provides more opportunities for upselling and cross-selling, which can lead to higher sales.

Analyze Your Best Sellers

- **Identify Top Performers**: Before adding new products, take the time to analyze your best-selling items. What products consistently sell out at events? Are there particular product categories that customers love? Use this data to guide your product development efforts.

- **Offer Variations**: You don't always need to introduce completely new products to expand your line. Sometimes offering variations of your best sellers, such as new colors, sizes, or flavors, can provide the diversity needed to attract a wider range of customers without drastically changing your production process.

Introduce Complementary Products

- **Complementary Items**: Expanding your product line with complementary items can enhance the customer experience and increase average transaction sizes. For example, if you sell handmade soap, you might add bath accessories like loofahs or towels. If you sell jewelry, consider offering storage options like jewelry boxes or travel pouches. These add-ons not only diversify your offerings but also create opportunities for bundling or gift sets.

Seasonal or Limited Edition Items

- **Limited-Time Offerings**: Offering seasonal or limited-edition products can create excitement and urgency for customers. For example, you might introduce holiday-themed products, seasonal flavors, or special editions of your best sellers. Limited-time items often drive impulse purchases, as customers feel compelled to buy before the product is no longer available.

3. Leveraging Online Platforms for Growth

Expanding your vending business beyond physical events by creating an online presence is essential in today's digital world. E-commerce offers an excellent opportunity to scale your business by reaching customers outside of vending events and providing an avenue for repeat sales.

Build an E-commerce Website

- **Your Own Online Store**: Building your own website with e-commerce functionality is a great way to control your brand and customer experience. Platforms like Shopify, Squarespace, or Wix make it easy to create an online store, even if you don't have technical expertise. Your website should reflect your branding, showcase your products, and make it easy for customers to place orders and contact you.

- **Use Online Marketplaces**: In addition to your own website, consider selling on online marketplaces like Etsy, Amazon Handmade, or eBay. These platforms have built-in audiences, which can help you reach new customers. However, it's important to understand the fees and competition associated with each platform before deciding where to sell.

Leverage Social Media for E-commerce

- **Social Media Shops**: Many social media platforms, like Instagram and Facebook, now offer built-in e-commerce tools. Setting up an Instagram or Facebook Shop allows your followers to browse and purchase your products directly from your social media profiles. This creates a seamless shopping experience and can increase your sales, especially among customers who discover your brand at vending events and want to make repeat purchases online.

Email Marketing for Retention

- **Build a Customer Email List**: One of the most effective ways to drive online sales and retain customers is through email marketing. If you've been collecting email addresses at vending events, you already have a valuable customer base that you can market to online. Use email newsletters to promote new product launches, share exclusive offers, and keep your customers engaged with your brand between events.

4. Expanding Geographically

As your business grows, you may want to consider expanding beyond your local market. Vending at events in new cities or regions can expose your business to a larger audience and increase your sales potential. However, geographic expansion comes with its own set of challenges, including higher travel costs and the need to adapt to different market preferences.

Start Small and Strategic

- **Test New Markets**: Before committing to large-scale geographic expansion, start by attending a few events in nearby cities or regions. This allows you to test the waters and gauge customer interest without taking on too much financial risk. Pay attention to customer preferences in different locations, as certain products may perform better in specific regions.

- **Track Your ROI**: When expanding to new locations, it's important to track the return on investment (ROI) for each event. Factor in travel costs, accommodation, booth fees, and any other expenses, and compare them to your sales. This will help you determine whether the event was profitable and whether it's worth attending future events in the same area.

Logistics of Travel and Expansion

- **Plan for Travel Costs**: Expanding to new regions often means higher travel costs, so plan accordingly. Consider the most cost-effective ways to transport your products, such as renting a van or working with a shipping company. Additionally, research accommodations, food, and other expenses ahead of time to stay within your budget.

- **Build Local Partnerships**: If you're vending in a new city, consider partnering with local businesses or vendors to increase your visibility. For example, you could collaborate with a local shop to sell your products in-store or cross-promote with other vendors at the event.

5. Managing Operational Challenges with Growth

As your business scales, you may face new operational challenges, from managing increased inventory to handling more complex logistics. Growth requires careful planning and the right tools to ensure that your business continues to run smoothly.

Inventory Management

- **Upgrade Your Systems**: As your product line grows, manual inventory tracking may no longer be sufficient. Consider upgrading to an inventory management software that integrates with your e-commerce platform and point-of-sale system. This will help you track stock levels in real-time, manage orders more efficiently, and reduce the risk of stockouts or overstocking.

- **Streamline Reordering**: As you scale, streamline your reordering process by building relationships with suppliers and setting up automatic restock alerts. Having a reliable system in place for reordering raw materials or finished products ensures that you can keep up with increased demand without running into delays.

Hiring Help

- **Bringing on Staff**: As your vending business grows, you may need to hire staff to help manage operations at events or assist with production, customer service, or shipping. Hiring employees or contracting temporary workers can relieve some of the pressure and allow you to focus on strategic growth.

Time Management

- **Outsource When Necessary**: Running a scaled business requires effective time management. Outsourcing certain tasks, such as website design, social media management, or bookkeeping, can free up time for you to focus on growth strategies. Identifying areas where your time is best spent allows you to optimize your efforts.

Conclusion: Scaling for Long-Term Success

Scaling your vending business is an exciting opportunity to grow your brand, increase your revenue, and reach new customers. However, it requires thoughtful planning and execution. Whether you're expanding to new locations, growing your product line, or leveraging online platforms, it's important to stay focused on your core strengths and build a scalable infrastructure that supports long-term success.

As your business continues to evolve, remember to track your progress, learn from each new venture, and stay adaptable to changing market trends and customer preferences. With the right approach, you can take your vending business to the next level and create a sustainable, thriving enterprise.

In conclusion, this eBook has provided a comprehensive guide on how to improve your vending opportunities—from laying the foundation of your business to scaling it for growth. By applying the strategies and insights shared in each chapter, you'll be well-equipped to navigate the challenges of vending and build a successful, profitable business that continues to grow and thrive.

CONCLUSION

YOUR PATH TO VENDING SUCCESS

Throughout this book, we've explored the various facets of running and growing a successful vending business. From understanding the fundamentals of vending and creating an eye-catching booth to handling challenges, navigating competition, and scaling for growth, you've gained a comprehensive guide to improving your vending opportunities.

Now, it's time to bring all of these concepts together. The key to long-term vending success lies in your ability to continuously adapt, refine your approach, and stay motivated in the face of challenges. This final chapter will recap the essential takeaways from the previous chapters and offer actionable insights to ensure that you can implement these strategies effectively.

Building a Strong Foundation

The first few chapters of this book focused on laying the foundation for a successful vending business. This foundation is crucial, as it determines how well you can grow and navigate the complexities of vending in a competitive environment.

Understanding the Basics

One of the primary steps to vending success is mastering the basics. Chapter 1 introduced the key elements that drive vending success, including having a quality product, ensuring strong customer engagement, and creating a visually appealing setup. These fundamentals are the pillars of any vending business and serve as a starting point for long-term growth.

The core elements of vending include:

- **Product Quality**: Offering high-quality, unique products that resonate with your target audience.

- **Customer Engagement**: Building strong relationships through excellent customer service and a welcoming booth environment.

- **Brand Consistency**: Ensuring your booth, products, and marketing materials reflect a cohesive and professional brand image.

Research and Event Selection

Choosing the right vending events is just as important as having a great product. Chapter 2 focused on the research and decision-making process that goes into selecting vending opportunities. Not every event will align with your target market or business goals, so it's essential to research each event carefully and understand its audience, size, and potential for profit.

Key takeaways for choosing events include:

- **Understand Your Audience**: Research the types of events your target customers attend, and make sure your products fit within the event's theme or focus.

- **Weigh the Costs**: Evaluate the costs of booth fees, transportation, and event-related expenses against the potential profit from sales.

- **Start Small and Build**: If you're new to vending or testing new markets, consider starting with smaller, local events before moving on to larger, high-traffic events.

Creating a Winning Setup and Engaging Customers

Once you've selected your events, your booth setup and customer interaction become critical elements in converting foot traffic into sales. Chapters 3 and 6 covered the importance of creating an eye-catching setup and effectively engaging customers.

Eye-Catching Booth Design

Your booth is your storefront, and first impressions matter. A well-designed booth can draw people in and set the tone for the customer experience. Chapter 3 emphasized the importance of having a clean, organized, and visually appealing booth that reflects your brand and encourages customers to browse your products.

Key points for a successful booth setup:

- **Visual Appeal**: Use color, lighting, and branding elements to make your booth stand out in a crowded marketplace.

- **Clear Signage**: Display pricing and product information clearly to avoid confusion and make it easy for customers to shop.

- **Interactive Elements**: Encourage customers to touch, try, or sample your products. The more interactive your booth is, the longer customers are likely to stay.

Engaging Customers

Customer engagement is not just about making sales; it's about creating a memorable experience that builds loyalty and encourages repeat business. Chapter 6 provided actionable tips on how to engage customers through active listening, asking open-ended questions, and making them feel welcome at your booth.

Key takeaways for customer engagement:

- **Approachable and Friendly**: Greet every passerby with a smile and make them feel comfortable. People are more likely to stop and engage when they feel welcomed.

- **Tailored Responses**: Personalize your responses to customer questions and preferences, and offer recommendations based on their needs.

- **Upsell and Cross-Sell**: Encourage customers to purchase complementary products by suggesting bundles or add-ons that enhance their purchase.

Overcoming Challenges and Navigating Competition

Every vendor faces challenges, whether it's bad weather, low foot traffic, or stiff competition from other vendors. In Chapters 7 and 9, we explored how to navigate these challenges with confidence and turn setbacks into opportunities for growth.

Navigating Competition

Chapter 7 covered strategies for standing out in a crowded marketplace. When faced with competition, it's essential to differentiate yourself through product quality, branding, and customer experience. Instead of fearing competition, use it as an opportunity to refine your approach and offer something unique.

Key strategies for navigating competition:

- **Focus on Unique Selling Points**: Highlight what makes your product special—whether it's the craftsmanship, materials, or design.

- **Competitive Pricing**: Be mindful of your competitors' pricing, but don't engage in a price war. Instead, emphasize the value and quality of your product.

- **Collaboration**: Build positive relationships with fellow vendors and consider collaboration opportunities, such as cross-promotions or bundling complementary products.

Handling Challenges

Chapter 9 dealt with common vending challenges, such as bad weather or low foot traffic. These setbacks are often outside of your control, but how you respond can make a big difference in the outcome. Flexibility, preparation, and a positive attitude are key to overcoming challenges and making the most of any vending event.

Key strategies for overcoming challenges:

- **Preparation**: Always bring extra supplies, backup equipment, and solutions for bad weather. Being prepared allows you to handle unexpected situations with ease.

- **Adaptability**: If the event isn't going as planned, adapt your approach. Offer special promotions, engage customers more personally, or collaborate with other vendors to boost foot traffic.

- **Learn from Setbacks**: Each challenge is an opportunity to learn and improve. Analyze what worked and what didn't, and use those insights to refine your strategy for future events.

Scaling for Growth

Once you've built a solid foundation, developed effective engagement strategies, and learned how to handle competition and challenges, the next step is scaling your business. Chapter 10 explored the key steps to growing your vending business, including expanding to new locations, diversifying your product offerings, and leveraging online platforms.

Expanding and Diversifying

Expanding your vending business involves attending larger events, entering new markets, and diversifying your product line. Growth requires careful planning and a willingness to take calculated risks, but it also offers significant opportunities to increase revenue and build brand recognition.

Key strategies for scaling your business:

- **Expand Geographically**: Consider vending at events in new regions or cities to reach a broader audience. Start small, track ROI, and build from there.

- **Diversify Products**: Introduce new products, variations, or complementary items to expand your offerings and appeal to a wider range of customers.

Leveraging E-Commerce

In addition to expanding through physical events, building an online presence is crucial for scaling your business. E-commerce allows you to reach customers outside of events and generate passive income between vending opportunities.

Key tips for leveraging e-commerce:

- **Build a User-Friendly Website**: Create a professional e-commerce website that showcases your products, provides an easy checkout experience, and integrates with your social media channels.

- **Use Social Media for Sales**: Set up social media shops on platforms like Instagram and Facebook to allow customers to browse and buy directly from your social profiles.

FINAL THOUGHTS

Growing a successful vending business requires a combination of strategy, resilience, and passion. By applying the concepts covered in this book—ranging from event selection and booth setup to marketing, overcoming challenges, and scaling—you are well-equipped to take your vending business to new heights.

Vending is a dynamic and rewarding field, but it requires continuous learning and adaptability. Stay open to feedback, embrace new opportunities, and keep refining your approach. As you grow, remember that the key to long-term success is building strong customer relationships, delivering exceptional products, and maintaining a commitment to excellence in everything you do.

With these tools and insights, you are ready to navigate the challenges of vending and grow your business with confidence. Keep moving forward, stay focused on your goals, and enjoy the journey as you continue to expand and thrive as a vendor.